CAREER CHANGE

*The Career Change
Roadmap to Live the Life
You Want and Do What
You Love*

K. ELIZABETH

©2016

Introduction

I want to thank you and congratulate you for choosing the book ***Career Change: The Career Change Roadmap to Live the Life You Want and Do What You Love.***

This book contains proven steps and strategies on how to identify your need for a career change and how to translate what you're most passionate about into the rewarding and fulfilling career you desire and deserve.

When we were children, we were asked what we wanted to be when we grew up. Some of us wanted to be world-renowned ballerinas while others wanted to work for NASA and fly to the moon. Some of us aspired to become doctors that would save hundreds of people or artists that would grace the world with our talent.

When we were in high school, we were asked again. For some, the childhood dream of going to outer space or saving people remained the same. For others exhausted by the now 10 or so years of schooling, their answers shifted away from school-intensive professions. Instead, they wanted to become an x-ray technician, a nurse, a teacher, a business owner, or an entrepreneur.

When we enrolled in college or entered the job market, we were asked again, only this time we were expected to know what we wanted to be. And of course, some of us did. Some of us enrolled in the appropriate college courses, landed internships that would give us experience in our field, and graduated in four years with strong network connections and a solid idea of where we wanted to work and what we wanted to do. For others, however, the idea of what we wanted to do was still unclear. So we picked a major that we thought we might like. We enrolled in classes, received our degree, and applied for a wide assortment of job openings hoping we might like where we ended up.

But whether you're the college graduate who knew exactly what you wanted to do or the individual who applied and hoped to find something you enjoyed, it would seem that you're now feeling a bit unsure of your choice.

Maybe the 8-5 office job you've worked at for years no longer offers the excitement and challenge you now crave, or the current company you work for doesn't value the same creativity you eagerly bring to business meetings. Perhaps you've reached the highest possible position in your career but still feel like it's not enough, or you can't seem to picture yourself doing what you're doing now 30 years down the road.

Whatever our career and age may be, many of us experience these feelings at least once in our careers, and that's perfectly okay. In fact, it's completely natural. When we grow as individuals, our values and aspirations change with us.

This book is intended for anyone who's recently been questioning their career choice or is actively seeking to change their career. We've dedicated each chapter to a different stage in this decision, from first identifying if a career change is right for you, pinpointing how drastic of a career change you desire, reflecting on what you value most, learning how to translate your passions into a career, beginning the actual process and what to expect, and finding resources that will help make the transition go smoother.

Thanks again for downloading this book. I hope you enjoy it!

Table of Contents

Chapter 1: Should You Change Your Career?

We'll be completely honest with you, changing your career is a *big* decision, but this doesn't necessarily mean it needs to be a hard one. With the right amount of patience, motivation, and self-reflection, the decision to change your career can oftentimes go on without a hitch. But before we delve into the questions you need to consider before changing your career and how you can successfully go about it, you'll first need to determine if changing your career is the right choice for you.

We stress the importance of identifying if you actually need to change your career because sometimes working under a despondent boss or in collaboration with an unmotivated coworker can make our career *seem* miserable. But when this happens, it can sometimes be because of the *people* around us, not the actual *career*. You might enjoy what you do, but when your coworker leaves you to do all the hard work, it can be hard to accurately gage your situation. Situations such as these, moreover, oftentimes require a change in scenery, not a change in our career. Sometimes all it takes is an office transfer to work under a new boss or a different coworker to work in collaboration with for projects.

So as you begin to think about a career change, make sure you consider your work environment. Is your boss the sole contributor to your distain for Monday mornings? Does the thought of a pesky coworker deflate your excitement for career-promoting projects at work? These are just two of the numerous questions you should consider as you begin to think about a career change. But to help this process go smoother, we've included a brief but effective career satisfaction survey that will help show why exactly you're seeking a career change.

Career satisfaction self-survey

This survey will take you about 5-10 minutes to complete, and is intended to help you identify your motivations for pursuing a career change. To get the best results, be sure to carefully consider and answer each question as honestly as you can. It's recommended that you avoid answering the questions mentally—if you're reading this on a Kindle, tablet, computer, or phone, take advantage of the tools available to you (Kindles, for example, have great highlighting functions that you can use to check off your answers with). If you're reading this book in paperback, we recommend using a pen or pencil to keep track of your answers.

Rate your answers using the 0-5 scale provided below. (**0** means completely false, **1.** means somewhat false, **2.** means slightly false, **3.** means slightly true, **4.** means somewhat true, and **5.** means completely true.)

1. I enjoy the challenges I'm faced with at work and am able to overcome them.

$$0 \quad 1 \quad 2 \quad 3 \quad 4 \quad 5$$

2. I've been given more responsibilities at work because of my hard-work and dedication, and I'm happy with it.

$$0 \quad 1 \quad 2 \quad 3 \quad 4 \quad 5$$

3. I'm able to use the skills and talents I value while at work.

O   1   2   3   4   5

4. I've been given or have found the right balance of freedom and structure in my career.

O   1   2   3   4   5

5. I've received a promotion somewhat recently (in the past couple of years).

O   1   2   3   4   5

6. I earn a salary that lets me live the lifestyle I want.

O   1   2   3   4   5

7. I often receive acknowledgement for my work and/or effort.

O   1   2   3   4   5

8. I feel motivated and inspired by the people I work for and/or with.

O   1   2   3   4   5

9. I feel my career has improved me as a person and as an employee.

      0   1   2   3   4   5

10. I feel I have made an impact on the company and/or those that I work with.

      0   1   2   3   4   5

11. I have made important connections with people.

      0   1   2   3   4   5

12. I have earned the respect of those around me and/or in my field.

      0   1   2   3   4   5

13. I am satisfied with my work-social life balance.

      0   1   2   3   4   5

14. I feel fulfilled.

      0   1   2   3   4   5

15. I'll be proud of the work that I've done even after I retire.

0   1   2   3   4   5

16. I enjoy talking about my career to others (at social gatherings or in general).

0   1   2   3   4   5

What your survey results tell you

Hopefully thinking about the survey's questions helped spark some ideas and important self-reflections on your career and your feelings toward it. But we want to make sure you fully understand what your results seem to tell you. With that being said:

- **Questions 1-4** target whether or not you're happy with your workload and if you're career allows you to apply the things you value most. Answering mostly 4 or 5s for these questions, for example, indicate that your career challenges you, supplies you with what you want, and encourages the application of the skills you value most. If your results show anything different, this may indicate that you feel restricted, overwhelmed, and unsatisfied— you're definitely in need of a career change.

- **Questions 5-8** are all about identifying if you are acknowledged, appreciated, and respected. Our careers oftentimes hinge upon the people we work with, so it's important that you experience these. If you don't, a career change should be in your future.

- **Questions 9-16** are self-reflection questions that get you thinking about how your career makes you feel. Feeling a sense of fulfillment and pride in your career is essential. Answering 0, 1, 2 and maybe even 3 might indicate your need for a career change—you don't want to look back on your career after you've retired and feel like it was a waste of time.

As you move forward with this book, keep in mind that:

- Being good at something is not the same as enjoying it.

- There is a difference between your career success (recent promotion, salary bump, being highly respected) and feeling fulfilled by your career.

- Going through a temporary rough patch at work does not necessarily mean you need a new career.

Chapter 2: What's Your New Career Path?

If you've completed the survey in Chapter 1 and still feel confident that you need a career change, the next step is to consider what exactly your career change should be. Can your career change be as simple as asking for an office or location transfer, or will your career change take you down an entirely untrodden path? Essentially, now's the time to decide: career tweak or complete career overhaul?

To discover your best course of action, identify the problem or the source behind your career dissatisfaction. Is your boss the reason why you hate coming to work and doing what you do? Well, this sounds like a career tweak. Finding a new boss to work under or switching work locations might be all you need to rediscover a love for what you do. Have you been feeling bored with your responsibilities and projects? Do you feel like your skills aren't being fully applied, that you're over-qualified, or that you're not encouraged or allowed to reach your full potential? These sounds like you're in need of a complete career overhaul.

Career Pathways

As you're thinking about your new career path, keep in mind the multitude of options you have in front of you. There are 6 major career pathways we can pursue:

- Arts and Communication

- Business, Marketing, Management, and Technology

- Engineering, Manufacturing, and Industrial Technology

- Health Sciences

- Human Services

- Natural Resources and Agri-science

Within each career pathway, there are a plethora of additional career routes you can explore and pursue. For example, if you value communication, appreciate one-on-one interactions, and strive to ensure clients are always happy with their product, whatever that may be, the Communication career path sounds like a good fit. Within this pathway alone are opportunities to pursue:

- Advertising and Public Relations

- Brand Manager

- College Admissions Representative

- Film Production

- Foreign Relations

- Grant Writing

- Graphic Arts

- Journalism

- Language Arts

- Office Manager for Medical or Dental Office

- Radio and Broadcasting

This is to name just a few. There are certainly a vast amount of other options, which can easily be found by utilizing a simple google search.

Career Income Opportunities

Career Pathway	Annual Estimated Income
Arts and Comunication	
Office Manager	$48,000
Public Relations Rep.	$61,500
Media Manager (TV, Radio)	$68,700
Business, Marketing, Management	
Hotel General Manager	$60,000
Construction Project Manager	$69,200
IT Project Manager	$95,000
Engineering, Manufactoring	
Electrical Engineering	$89,180
Computer Engineering	$150,130
Petroleum Engineering	$132,000
Health Services	
Radiation Therapist	$77,340
Physician's Assistant	$84,830
Pharmacist	$106,630

As you start to make these decisions, there are a few things you should keep in mind along the way. The first is that regardless of the career path you choose to pursue, you should make sure that you'll be able to apply the skills you have without restriction and that you'll value what you do. The second idea to keep in mind may not be as important to some, but it's definitely a driving factor for most—money. Your new career path, whether it's a tweak or overhaul—should help you achieve a place you feel comfortable with money-wise. If this is an important factor for you, it's crucial that you do your research as you ponder new careers. This is because some career pathways inevitable lead to better success than others. The science industry, for example, is booming right now because our society values exponential growth, technological break-throughs, and is focused on discovering treatments and cures for illnesses and diseases. You'll find that many of the careers down this pathway offer a starting salary much higher than other career pathways. Check out the brief but illuminating chart that shows examples of what we mean (left). Although there are some excellent high-income career opportunities in the Communication field, you'll find that incomes in the Engineering field are simply higher because these jobs are in high demand.

Chapter 3: Before You Change Careers

Changing our career revolves around careful considerations—why do I want to change my career? How drastic should my change be? What career path do I want to pursue instead? How will my new career path allow me to incorporate my skills and talents while earning an income that supports me? Asking yourself these questions is great. But there's another step to the process before you change your career, and that's self-reflecting.

In order for you to successfully switch your career, you first need to fully understand what you're looking for in your new endeavors. This means dedicating some time to discovering what you truly enjoy, value, and seek. This is crucial because your assessment and self-reflection will serve as your career compass. If you don't know what you value, you might end up with another career that just doesn't reward you in the way you want or help you feel fulfilled.

Reflection questions: What do you value?

To help you begin this crucial pre-career change self-reflection, we've included a few suggestions on things to consider:

- What do you value? (Creativity, independence, lose structure, strict deadlines, close collaborations?)

- What skills do you have that set you apart from others? If you answered that you don't have any, how can you turn your skills into something unique?

- How can you make your skills look most appealing to future employers?

- How do you like to work? In what environment? (Surrounded by people, in private area with a few close coworkers? Independently?)

- Where/how do you want to work? (For a Fortune 500 company, a family business, or self-employed?)

- What do you love to do in your free time?

- How can you apply what you love to do in your free time to the environment you want to work in?

- What other work-related preferences do you have, if any?

- What would you want to do, even if you weren't paid for it?

- If the world didn't impose any restrictions, what would your career be?

- Will you keep your current job as you search for a new career, or will you dedicate all of your attention to the career change process?

Asking yourself these questions and answering them as honestly as you can will give you some idea of who you are as a career-driven individual. Someone might reflect that they value unrestricted creativity, complete independence, and strict deadlines, for example. Through these self-reflection exercises, this individual may come to realize that they want to pursue a career in the Arts where they have the freedom to create without limitations. Or, if someone has worked for a Fortune 500 company for the past 20 years, is extremely charismatic, loves working collaboratively, and enjoys watching Shark Tank in his or her free time, the business career pathway might be a good choice.

The point is, we can't fully, effectively, or productively pursue something if we don't know what we want to get out of it. A career change involves your dedication to self-reflection and discovering what you truly value and appreciate. Your career is something you should look forward to, not something that you simply wake up and *do,* so it's very important that you think about a career in which you can easily incorporate what you love into it.

Your mindset and attitude

The success of our career change depends on our dedication to reflecting on what we value and want in a career, but it also hinges upon our mental mindset and attitude. Confidence and resilience are especially important during this process.

- **Confidence:** When we say confidence, we mean believing that you can accomplish the task at hand and, moreover, accomplish it well. If you want to successfully change your career, confidence is crucial. You need to know and believe that you have the skills necessary to succeed at whatever career you may choose. Your display of confidence will also assure potential employers that you can bring to their team unparalleled skills, unwavering motivation, and a strong work ethic.

- **Resilience:** Despite our confidence, however, we sometimes face minor speed bumps during our career change process. But with resilience—the ability to recover quickly and overcome difficulties—these set-backs will become fleeting matters.

Chapter 4: Translating What You Love into a Career

So you've spent some time discovering what you value, appreciate, and love. Now what? How can you possibly make your self-reflections translate into a career you enjoy?

Considering potential employers and clients

After you've established what you can passionately bring to your career, what you enjoy doing, and what type of environment you want to work in, the next step is to work out how you can transfer your interests and loves into a rewarding, fulfilling, and supporting career. To successfully do this, we should familiarize ourselves with a few important elements—we need to:

- Know what hiring companies/employers/clients in our field look for and appreciate

- Learn what skills and experience employers will require of us

Our best suggestion is **research, research, research**. You want to find a career that will let you incorporate what you value and do what you love, right? Well, you'll need to find an employer who will let you do this (unless you're planning on taking the self-employed route), and this means finding out what potential employers value and appreciate. If you aspire to work for a popular or large company, for example, performing a google search and finding their website online is often a big help. Almost all company websites will have an "About Us," an "Our Mission," or a "Careers" link that will clearly outline who the founders are, what the company does, and, most importantly for your situation, what the company and the company's CEOs and management staff value most. If your values don't mirror theirs, move on. There's always another career opportunity.

More self-reflection

After you've narrowed down your career path and have done some research on what potential employers or clients value, it's time for more consideration and reflection. This time, with your employer's values in mind, honestly consider if your skills and desires will be a good fit. Some helpful things to think about are:

- o **Job prospects:** If you're career-driven, you most likely want to find a job that offers frequent promotions, opportunities for salary bumps, great healthcare and insurance benefits, and perhaps even travel opportunities. If you greatly value these elements, make sure you do your research and/or ask questions about these employment prospects during interviews. You've already spent so much time considering and looking for a new career—you don't want to end up in a career that you'll get bored with within a year or feel stuck with.

- o **Work-life balance:** You can land the perfect career, but the glow of your new job can quickly fade if it becomes too demanding or you feel like your social life is affected by it. If you value a balance between work and your non-work life, be sure to ask questions about what type of hours are required *and* expected. Sometimes you'll find that some careers require 40 hours of work a week, but that employees are expected to put in an additional 10 hours of their own time. Remember, you can love your career but still love your free time as well. Get answers to these questions before your settle down with your new career.

Chapter 5: Career Change Tools and Suggestions

Once you've identified your reasons for wanting to change careers, have reflected upon what you value most in a career, and have thought about how you will approach translating your interests into a rewarding career opportunity, you're ready to begin the actual career change process. A word of caution, however—this certainly is a process. For some, switching careers might take a week. For others, finding the career you *desire* and *deserve* might take months, even years. But you shouldn't let this hold you back from beginning the actual process. Changing our career requires patience and dedication, but it also requires us to actively act upon what we want. Fortunately, there are numerous ways in which you can productively speed the career change process up. Take some time to read the following highly effective tools and suggestions for beginning your career change and ensuring you find your ideal career in as little time as possible.

Career change tools

- **Take advantage of Facebook and LinkedIn:** These are two highly effective social media sites that oftentimes produce great results for those looking to change their careers. Perhaps one of your old high school friends recently started a marketing business and has written a Facebook post explaining his search for a graphic designer—this is a perfect opportunity for the independent artist looking to channel their talent into a more professional setting. Or, if you have an idea of what career field you'd like to pursue, you can post a status to see if anyone has heard of any recent openings. Let your friends help you—you'll be surprised just how many helpful comments show up on your post. If you're looking for a more professional environment, however, LinkedIn is a great resource as well. It's similar to Facebook in that you can stay connected to colleagues and classmates, but you can also build your own professional profile that employers can browse and review. It's a great resource for discovering professional opportunities and new ventures, but it's also riddled with helpful links about tips that will surely help you pursue the career you want.

- **Involve others:** One of the most common mistakes we make when changing careers is cutting people out of the process, whether accidently or intentionally. Sometimes we fear that we'll be treated differently if our coworkers know about our career change. But if you're in search of a new career because the company you work for doesn't appreciate you, you can usually expect that others feel the same way, too. Be open with coworkers that you are friendly with and feel comfortable talking to. They can sometimes give you a perspective you hadn't thought about before, make suggestions based on their view of your work, and help you with the networking process. You might even find that they're in the same situation as you. We also encourage you to discuss your career change with family and friends. These are the people who know you best, and they're also the ones you should trust. Confide in them, ask for their advice, and embrace their suggestions. Sometimes we can become so overwhelmed by this process that we don't see things as clearly as we should.

- **Analyze, but also act:** No matter how many nights you stay up late conducting research on potential employers or the amount of charts, lists, graphs, Venn diagrams, and pros and cons lists you make, you're never going to successfully change your career until you act. Although we do encourage all of the above, you at some point need to make your decision and actively pursue it. There's a certain amount of time required for thinking over our decisions, but there's also a specific time for acting. Don't drag your feet. Do research, find a good match, and then full-heartedly dive into it without looking back.

Further suggestions

- **Look for people:** This might come as a surprise to some people, but when you're looking for your future career, look for the people you want to work with. If you're seeking the self-employed route this may not be as relevant, but for all those planning to pursue almost all other career paths, this is important. Our career satisfaction is based largely on the people we're surrounded by. Our bosses, coworkers, clients, and customers play a major role in how we view our careers. Decide *what* you want to do, *which* environment you want to work in, and *who* you want to work with. Surrounding yourself with like-minded people who appreciate and value the same things you do is an excellent way to decide if a career opportunity will be a perfect match.

- **Don't look into "hot" career paths unless you're truly interested and it's a good fit:** Like we saw in Chapter 2, there are some career pathways that are drastically more active than others. Careers in Science or Technology almost always have higher starting salaries than those of Communication or Human Services, for example. However, it's important that you don't let the thought of money alone draw you into a career. Your next career should be something you're passionate about and enjoy doing—money can be a factor during your search, but it shouldn't dictate what pathways you choose to further investigate and pursue.

- **Sometimes going back to school isn't the answer:** While career pathways such as Health Services generally require at least 4 years of schooling, the Arts pathway doesn't always require a degree to be successful. Instead, your career opportunities are usually based upon internships, experiences, and clients. So, don't think that you *need* to go back to school. Sometimes you can save a lot of money and time by finding internships, volunteer work, or freelance work in your field, which oftentimes lead to networking and career connections.

Chapter 6: What To Expect

Sometimes we struggle with the decision to change our career because we fear uncertainty. We worry about what we'll do during the career change process, we inevitable question our decision to switch careers as we dangle in between them, and we stress about what will happen after we have made the switch. This chapter is for anyone who is experiencing the feelings of uncertainty and anxiety slowly creeping in. Our first suggestion? Relax. Take a deep breathe. Stop stressing. The things we feel passionately about always have a way of working themselves out. Motivation, dedication, patience, and persistence are incredibly powerful attributes essential to the career change process. If you're still worried, here's a short (but hopefully stress-reducing) list of what to expect during and after you've made your career change:

- **Happiness:** After all, didn't you make the change because your career was unrewarding or left you with a feeling of being unfulfilled? For many who have made a successful career change, Mondays are no longer a dreaded day of the week and getting out of bed in the morning isn't as hard as it once was (although, for us non-morning people, it might still be a pain). You should finally feel excited to go to work, interact with others, and overcome hurdles.

- **Transition period:** It's important that you keep this in mind: you may need to allow some time to transition into your new career, especially if you've made a dramatic change.

Starting a new career is an exciting time, but it's also a time full of changes and learning new things. Be sure to give yourself reasonable time to adjust.

- **Slow start:** This idea speaks especially to those who have followed the career path of self-employment or entrepreneurship. Whether you're starting up a business or selling products, business will, without a doubt, be relatively slow. Establishing yourself, your brand, or your project(s) is a process that takes time. Be dedicated, be honest, and, most importantly, be patient. We sometimes feel the urge to give up when our expectations aren't fully met—don't. You've already put so much time into changing your career, so give it just a little more time.

Chapter 7: Further Recommendations

Hopefully you've been able to find some helpful pieces of information as you've read this book. To further ensure your career change process goes smoothly, we've included multiple additional resources that you can consult and take advantage of as you search for new careers or work on those sometimes dreadful resumes and CVs.

Career search engines

If you haven't paid attention to the job market recently, you'll be surprised to know just how often potential employers utilize the internet and social media platforms when job openings arise or when they conduct background checks on potential employees and interviewees. And because more and more employers are flocking toward technology as a means to browse and find potential employees, more and more websites have been created to help *you* find *them*. We recommend two:

1.) Monster.com: You can upload your resume for employers to browse, find helpful tips on writing your cover letter and resume, search for *any* type of job, browse a list of the most popular jobs, and explore the different career communities you can easily become a part of. Essentially, Monster.com is all about reaching out to potential employers, making connections, and bettering yourself as an applicant and career-driven individual. Plus, Monster's software and page layout is extremely easy to use for career-seekers of all ages.

2.) Indeed.com: Indeed.com's layout isn't as visually pleasing as Monster's, but it still gets the job done—no pun intended. You'll come across a simple page that lets you enter what job you're looking for and in what geographical area. You can control the search result by changing the radius, selecting your desired salary estimate, and choosing the specific company name, if you have some in mind. We'd recommend this site if you're unfamiliar with the search engine tool or find that Monster.com's options and opportunities are just a little too overwhelming.

Resume and CV Resources

If you've been out of the job market for a while—even for a couple years—your resume and CV most likely need an update. These documents are crucial items as you begin your search for your perfect career, so you want them to be as up-to-date, professional, and accessible as possible. So, where do you start? Well, we'd recommend:

1. Quintessential Careers: Quint Careers takes the form of a blog/website hybrid. It's a clean, simple, and easy-to-use website managed by Dr. Randall S. Hansen who is invested in helping career-driven individuals find their ideal career in as painless of a way as possible. You'll find that it's loaded with helpful tips and templates for all things career-related, from resume templates, resume builders, resume examples, resume samples, tips on how to compose a cover letter, and suggestions on what not to include on your resume or CV. We highly recommend browsing through the materials, but to save you some time, we've included a few links that will bring you directly to some of Hansen's most helpful and effective information:

- Resumes building:
  http://www.quintcareers.com/resres/

- Cover letter composing:
  http://www.quintcareers.com/covres/
- Interviewing tips:
  http://www.quintcareers.com/intvres/

Remember, finding your perfect career isn't solely about reflecting on what you want and doing research on potential career pathways and employers. It's also about transforming yourself into the best and most qualified candidate for the job. You'll be able to discuss your qualifications and passions for your career during your interview, but you need your resume or CV to get past an employer's screening process first—your resume is your initial introduction. It's important that you (truthfully) make yourself shine on it.

Conclusion

A career change can be a stressful and long-winded process, but it doesn't have to be. Discovering whether a career change is right for you can be answered by reflecting on your values as an individual and familiarizing yourself with the multitude of career pathways and branches. But remember, you won't land your ideal career unless you act upon your self-reflections and research. There will come a point where charts, graphs, Venn diagrams, and pros and cons lists just won't get the job done anymore. In other words, with the right combination of *reflection* and *action* you'll be able to translate your passions and values into a career that is rewarding and fulfilling.

Thank you again for downloading this book! I hope this book helped you gain confidence and a better understanding for the career change process and helped you move toward the life you want and a career you feel passionate about. If you haven't already done so, the next step is to put this book done and apply what you've learned here to your career change.

Finally, if you enjoyed this book, would you be kind enough to leave a review for this book on Amazon? It'd be greatly appreciated

Thank you!

K. Elizabeth

Made in the USA
San Bernardino, CA
01 July 2016